Another

sad
mad
glad
book

The Anatomy of Your Attitude

Chuck Stump & Jim Strawn

Another Sad Mad Glad Book-The Anatomy of Your Attitude

For permissions, to order additional copies of this title, or to contact the authors, call or write:

Four Dolphins Press, LLC
P. O. Box 833, Scott Depot, West Virginia, 25560
Phone (304) 757-8125

Visit our Web site at www.fourdolphins.net

Printed in the United States of America
First Edition: September 2008

ISBN: 978-0-9799315-2-9

Four Dolphins Press would like to give the following people a pat on the back for lending a helping hand.

Graphic Design: Michael Teel - Progressity, Inc., Charleston, WV
Contributing Photographers: Steve Payne. Bruce and Linda Wollaber
Editor: Nancy Wallace
Creative Consultant: Brendan Stump
JE Robins Elementary, Charleston, WV - Grades 3, 4 and 5, 2008
Weberwood Elementary, Charleston, WV - Grades 3,4 and 5, 2008
West Teays Elementary, Hurricane, WV - Grades 3, 4 and 5, 2008

Dedicated to Joe. Our "right hand man."

Our mentor. Our friend.

Our first book took us

head to toe,

but still there's lots to learn.

So you'll find more lessons in this book

with every page you turn.

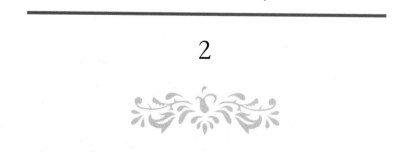

Our animal friends are back for more,

so you know it won't be boring.

They'll teach us what we need to know

to keep our attitudes soaring!

Some lessons from the first book
are so strong they're worth repeating.
One thing we learned was win or lose,
we **shake hands**
after competing.

We learned to

put our best foot forward

and to

lend a helping hand.

We learned to have

a heart of gold

and that sharing is just grand!

We hope you've learned to
bite your tongue.

If not, here's a reminder.

Unpleasant thoughts should not be said.

Work hard on being kinder.

We learned to smile when with

our friends and how to

give someone a lift.

To

**get down on our
knees and pray...**

for each day is a special gift.

Enough review – let's move ahead!

We won't go **head to toe.**

Let's say we're going to

play it by ear!

Get ready! Here we go!

Read this book with an **eagle eye,**

and when you're finished you'll be smart.

Study the rhymes and pictures and

take each lesson to heart.

If you **stay on your toes**

while reading this book,

you'll be focused and paying attention.

You'll make parents (and teachers!) very

GLAD

and improve your comprehension.

But if **your heart isn't in it**,

your interest is low.

You'll be bored or just plain lazy.

When you **let your mind wander**,

your attention is poor.

That drives parents and teachers crazy.

Have you ever had a **bad hair day?**

It's no cause for

SAD or **MAD.**

Just **keep your nose to the grindstone**

and focus on being

GLAD!

Good listeners remember what they hear.

Poor listeners…they don't bother.

They simply let the message go

in one ear and out the other.

You can talk to them until you're
blue in the face,
but they still don't seem to listen.

It really is an awful shame

because they don't know what they're missin'.

Finally someone

gives you an earful,

and that just creates more tension.
When everything is said and done
you'll wish you'd been paying attention.

**When was the last time someone
gave you an earful?**

If you **listen to your elders**,

you'll succeed in fewer tries.

They've been down the road you travel,

and their mistakes have made them wise.

Where do you go for help or advice?

Grown-ups
**have eyes in the
backs of their heads**
that give them a perfect view.

So don't try to
pull the wool over their eyes.
They already know what's true.

And when they **roll their eyes** and stare,

you'll know that you've been busted.

You need to be honest and tell the truth

if you ever want to be trusted!

It's easy to remember what you said
if you always tell the truth.
You'll even remember it years from now
when you're really

long in the tooth!

When a grown up says, "There's work to do!"

you should do it right away.

If you lolly-gag, or

drag your feet,

There won't be time to play.

With some

elbow grease,

or effort,

the work will soon be done.

And now it's time for your reward.

Go play and have some fun!

Fear is a feeling everyone knows.

It's called being

weak in the knees.

What are you afraid of --

could it be heights, or snakes or bees?

Some say when you're

MAD

your **blood boils,**

Others say they're

seeing red.

Your temper is something

that you can control.

Learn to

keep a level head.

Butting heads

is something else that's bad.

It's a game no one can win.

It's best to try to work things out

before someone

takes one on the chin!

Speaking of chins, it's best to
keep your chin up.

It's a habit that can be taught.

You can **get a leg up** on

SAD and **MAD**

once you master this powerful thought.

Most bullies don't use fists,

but **WORDS,**

to intimidate and hurt.

Be aware and watch out for your friends.

Always be on the alert.

Bullies might be girls or might be boys.

Either gender may be an offender.

But when you stand strong beside your friends,

bullies usually surrender.

We all need to **have an open mind,**
to learn "What?" and "How?" and "Why?"
It's important that we get along.
That's **seeing eye-to-eye.**

Keep your hands to yourself.

That's a very good rule.

It shows respect for your friends,

both at home and at school.

"Shake a leg!"

is something parents say,

when the family is running late.

Be ready when it's time to go,

so others won't have to wait.

Expensive things cost

an arm and a leg.

Is there something that you're craving?

"A penny saved is a penny earned."

That's Ben Franklin's rule on saving!

Are you saving money for something special?

But heed this warning about money and stuff.

There will **always** be someone with more.

Count relationships and what you give.

That's a much better way to keep score!

Here's the sphinx. He lives in Egypt.

He's here to help us make a point.

He shows us just how bad we look

when our

nose gets out of joint.

If you've bitten off more than you can chew, your eyes were bigger than your stomach, I'm guessin'. Now you find yourself in over your head. Pay attention and look for the lesson.

Your **right hand man** is the one you trust
when it's time to work as a team.
He or she will give you that extra thrust
when it seems like you're paddling upstream.

Who is your "right hand man?"

Moss grows on rocks and trees and things because they never move, but

moss will not grow under your feet

as long as you work to improve.

If you study a lesson or practice a skill,
after a while you **know it by heart.**
With **ice in your veins,**
you'll take center stage
and calmly perform your part.

A friend might tell you,

"Break a leg!"

Don't worry; it's just an expression.

It's a special way to say, "Good luck!

Go make a good impression!"

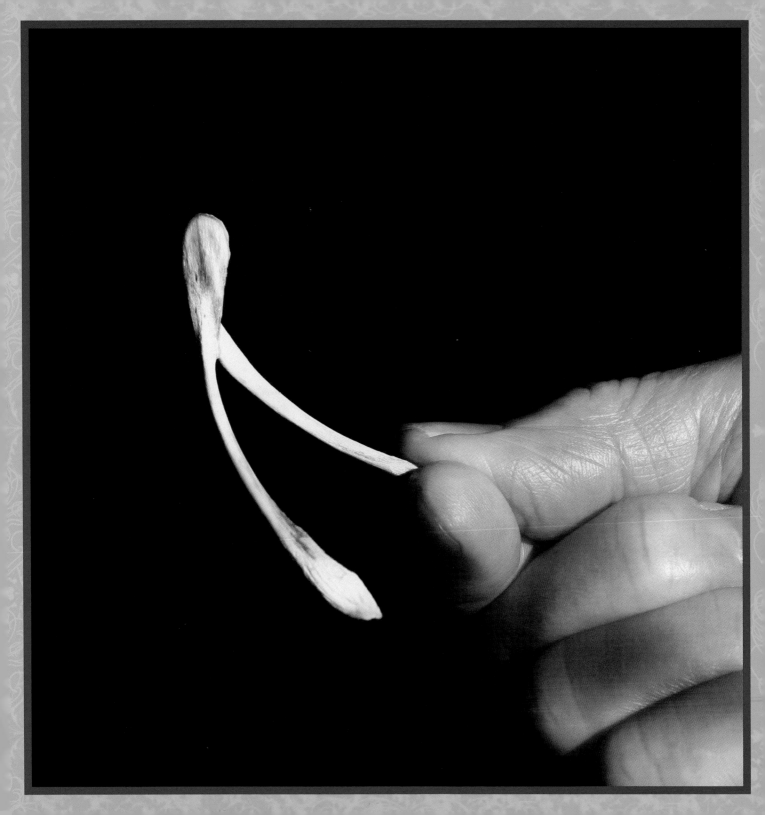

This one's for parents everywhere

with kids who win a prize.

You can still cheer loud with that

lump in your throat

and those

tears that fill your eyes!

When the compliments and praise start flowing,
be humble -- don't get the

BIG head.

A smile, and a wink, and a "thank you" are best.

That's all that needs to be said.

You know you have five senses --
hearing, sight, touch, taste and smell.
But there's talk about a **sixth sense,**
one you might not know so well.

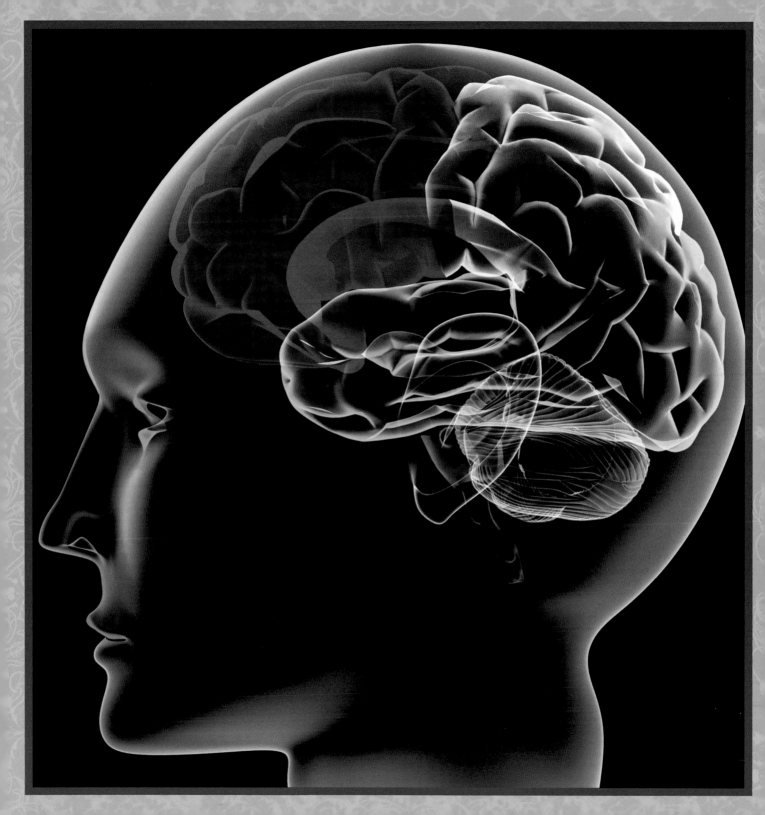

Sometimes you

feel it in your bones

or you

feel it in your gut.

You might hear a

voice inside your head

and think you're going nuts!

As Shakespeare said in **Hamlet**,

"To thine own self be true."

Trust your soul

and learn to listen.

Follow your heart

and take your cue.

If you

stick out like a sore thumb,

you're only different from the rest.

That doesn't mean that something's wrong.

Who knows? You might be best!

Once you've made the right decision,
it will **take your breath away.**
You'll have a place to **sink your teeth**
and work will seem like play.

Time and tide wait for no man,

and we all know that time does fly.

For life comes at you very fast

and is gone in the

blink of an eye.

Your journey lies before you.

You have people to meet and mountains to climb.

Keep a **smile on your face**

and good **thoughts in your head,**

and live life **one step at a time.**

So when you're

on your last leg

and you're ready to quit,

and

you've worked your fingers to the bone...

Look down the road with a sense of pride, knowing finally… it's time to go home.

The End

We would like to know what you think.
Go to www.fourdolphins.net and send
us your Book Report.

Thanks!

Chuck   *Jim*